To Hell and Back

An Autobiography of an
International Football Player

Errol Anthony Stevens

Editor & Publisher:

www.hcpbookpublishing.com
info@hcpbookpublishing.com

Book and Cover design by HCP Book Publishers

ISBN-13: 978-1720938873
ISBN-10: 1720938873

First Edition: 2018

I want to dedicate this book to my parents, Errol Anthony Stevens Snr. and Arlene Stevens.

Also, to my grandparents, wife, Ekaterina Nikiforova Stevens, and my two lovely boys, Lionel and Daniel Stevens.

Acknowledgments

I want to thank Cleveland O. McLeish, CEO of HCP Book Publishing, for accepting this project and giving me a chance to do something that was only a thought. With your help, this book has become a reality, and I know this is only the beginning.

I want to thank my parents, grandparents, aunt, and uncles who all raised me. I was lucky and blessed to have so many God-fearing people in my young life that made me the man I am today.

Special thanks to my wife. I love you with all my heart. Thank you for believing in me, and my story is what it is because of you. You saw something in me that very few people saw.

To my sons, Lionel and Daniel. You are my driving force, and because of you guys, I want the world and everything in it so that I can pass it on to you.

Table of Contents

When one door is closed,
don't you know another is open?

(From the Song,
"Coming in From the Cold" by Bob Marley)

Introduction

One day I was having a discussion with some of my friends who also play football, and I realized there are people who support what I do, but there will always be some who talk behind my back. They will say I have changed because of where I am now, but I know I haven't. I have always been an introvert who prefers to stay in my own corner, doing my own thing and playing football.

I was sharing with my friends that the same people who criticised us for making use of the opportunities when they come will not be hungry enough to go after a similar opportunity if it is presented to them. I have seen talented footballers get a chance and allow it to slip through their fingers because the process looked too hard or the dream too impossible to fulfill.

I don't like to blow my own horn, but I have helped people along my own journey. In 2016, I visited Jamaica and connected with two football players who had been messaging me constantly because they wanted an opportunity to play professional football. They said nothing was happening for them in Jamaica, so I told my agent about them. They were as big and fast as I was, and they could play football just as good. I took them as far as to sign contracts with my agent before I left Jamaica.

When I spoke with the agent, he said he would be sending for one. He asked me to pick the one who I thought was more hungry for the opportunity, so I did. The player came to Vietnam. He saw me living a certain quality of life and thought that it would come easy. I worked for what I have, and maybe I gave the impression that it was easy to live the kind of life I was living, but it wasn't. It came as a result of great sacrifice and literally going through hell. I have never gone public with my full story, until now.

My life is not perfect – and no one's life is. People show you what they want you to see, so if you see me eating at a fancy restaurant, that doesn't mean I don't also eat food that is 'not that good' sometimes. But at the end of the day, I grew up in Jamaica, and I was used to certain things in life. We should not make a habit of judging people by where they are, because we don't know how they got there and the price they had to pay.

So I sent for the player, and he immediately started complaining about the food. This is Vietnam – not Jamaica – the food is going to taste different. I understood that and never made a big deal out of it. I came from a place where I had nothing, so a difference in taste doesn't bother me. As long as the food doesn't kill me, I can handle it.

Every single day, the player complained about the food. I kept telling him that when the contract is signed, and he starts earning, he would be able to buy what he wants to eat.

Then he started complaining about the firmness of the bed. Another friend who migrated the same time I did mentioned how tough the bed was when we first got there, but we never complained and didn't let it bother us.

People back home say those of us who make it out of whatever bad positions we were in are never willing to help others do the same. The truth is, we do want to help, but sometimes it's not as easy as it sounds. It is not a bed of roses.

I know a lot of players who come here complaining about the same things. Sometimes they are the same people talking about us. The friend I recommended came here but ended up going home after only a week. I felt bad because I was the one who recommended this player to the agent. I even offered to pay for his ticket.

I was so upset about the situation that I didn't follow through with the second player I had recommended. I think they expect it to be easy, but it is not. We must be willing to work for what we want and not expect it to be handed to us on a silver platter.

I share my story with the hope of inspiring those who dare to dream big. I can tell you that if you are willing to put in the work and make the necessary sacrifices, you can make it. No dream is beyond your reach, really, and those who fail are those who give up.

There are some significant people I want to mention in telling my story because I recognize that my journey is as much theirs as it is mine. We cannot achieve success alone. We need a strong support system—those who will encourage us when we contemplate surrender and giving up. Even though some people still give up with a support system, they played a major part in my growth and development as a football player, a husband, and a father. I learned responsibility and discipline from those who came into my life and stayed for the long haul.

I hope my story inspires you to go after your dreams and never give up. Also, learn to appreciate the important people who are placed in your life and ignore the naysayers. There is greatness in you but many obstacles to overcome on your journey to becoming great.

CHAPTER 1

Humble Beginnings

My mom is my hero, but she was also known as the 'fiery one.' I have the uttermost respect for my parents when reminiscing about my life growing up. I remember it all. We lived in Portmore Lane, which was also known as "Don Land." One may consider that community as one of the worst squatter's land in Portmore, St. Catherine back then.

My grandparents ran away from the garrison community known as Trench Town during the war between the People's National Party (PNP) and the Jamaica Labour Party (JLP). The two opposing governmental sects were known to provoke war among the common people who were willing to fight and kill anyone who was wearing the wrong color shirt.

I was born in 1986. We lived in a big yard with my grandparents. My parents had a small board house right next door to theirs.

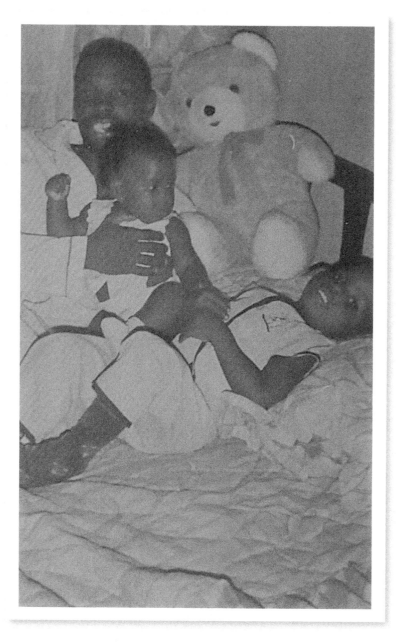

My Dad, Errol Stevens Snr., in our board home in
Portmore Lane. Happier days.

My Mom, Arlene Stevens, the strongest woman I know. We were celebrating Christmas in our little happy home in Portmore lane.

Mom and Day, happy days.
This is picture perfect, how I like to think of them.

My mom and dad argued a lot back then, and I still remember the day they decided to go their separate ways. During that time, Mom destroyed my dad's car during one of their arguments. The rest is history. They were in the process of buying a home in Greater Portmore, and I guess that family dream turned into a nightmare. Mom moved me and my sister to Greater Portmore. She was so broken that, on several occasions, I had to stop her from attempting to kill herself. I understood her predicament. She was a single mom with no job and two young children.

Mom found a way to raise two great children, even though we had to endure a lot. Mom didn't have a job, so most of the time she would travel on her visa to the United States and hustle, so we didn't have her around a lot. She would be overseas most of the time, and she did it for us. While she was away, we would be left with someone willing to care for us. Sometimes it was grandma, sometimes my mom's friends, sometimes a friend would get paid to keep us. At the end of Mom's 'hustling,' she would pack barrels and send them back home. That part we enjoyed.

Our lives became unstable without Dad around, but we did manage to go to prep school, so at least we had the option of getting a good education. Dad took care of that part. When we didn't have enough money for school, Mom encouraged us to sell sweats she had brought from overseas at school. That was illegal in prep school, and my sister didn't want any part of it. I didn't care as much, so I did it.

I was always willing to do honest work to survive. As long as I wasn't stealing, I was fine with whatever opportunity presented itself.

The three of us lived in a very small room. It was uncomfortable, but it was home. We lived there all the way through high school. I don't practice ingratitude for how I grew up, because all the experiences I had helped to make me the person I am today. Mom was always willing to move the world for us, and we appreciated her for her many selfless sacrifices. She fulfilled her role as a parent and helped me to be the kind of father I am today to my two boys, Lionel and Daniel. It is the burden of parents to take care of their children. You can't tell a two-year-old to go get a job to feed themselves or to pay bills. That is a parent's job. I have no idea how Mom did it, but she did. Children don't bring themselves into this world, so unless parents play their role as best as they can, a child cannot survive. Every child that survives long enough to make their own decisions have some parent or parent figure to thank because that means someone took them through the years that they could not take care of themselves.

My mom is my hero. Now, let's talk about football.

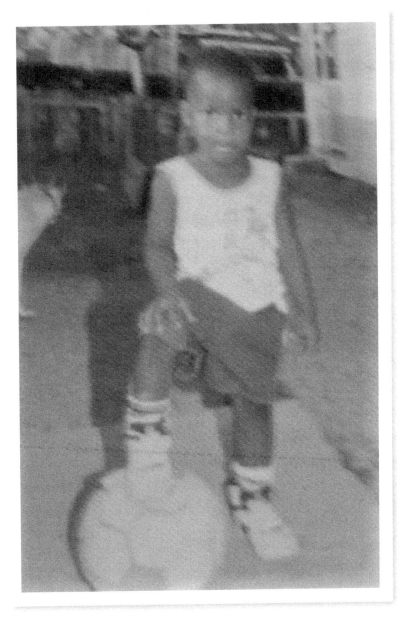

This is me at three years old in Portmore Gardens.

Me and my sis, Jody-Ann, about to leave home for work.
This was me working as an accountant.

My lovely grandmother, Victoria Stevens.
She laid a godly foundation for my life.

This is Ferdinand and Victoria Stevens, my grandparents.

CHAPTER 2

Getting My Foot in the Door

Sometimes humble beginnings provoke us to dig deep and find some intrinsic ability, skill, or passion that we can develop and attach ourselves to. For a lot of young men growing up in the inner city, and lacking the necessities of life growing up, that ability is music. For others, it is sports. I liked football from the first day my foot encountered a ball. But my journey into football did not officially begin until my first professional contract started. Until that point, football was a passion and a fun past time.

It started locally in Jamaica in 2009 with Harbour View FC. I had just finished playing under-21's for the youth team in Harbour View, and I did so well, that I was moved up to the Premier League team. I was so excited.

Helped Harbour view FC to their first under-21 title in the club history.

Back then, every young man's dream was to play for Harbour View, and every child knew that Ricardo 'Bibi' Gardner (International Jamaica Football Player) came through Harbour View. Gardner helped Jamaica to qualify for the World Cup in 1998. Watching that game made me realize I wanted to be a footballer, but I needed to get my foot in the door.

As a Jamaican child, I knew I could make a living out of football and Gardner, who played on the Reggae Boyz team, opened that door for most of us back when Jamaica first qualified for the World Cup. In 1998, he was signed to play for the Bolton Wanderers Football Club in England. He stayed with them for fourteen years. Watching him play in England for Bolton really gave me that push, and I told myself that one day I would be playing football outside of Jamaica.

When the opportunity was given to me for a chance to play for Harbour View, it was a dream come true, but not all dreams start as dreams. I was a new kid among a group of stars. I was with players like Fabian Taylor – one of my idols – and many more. There was Richard Edward, Donald Stewart, Kavin Bryan – so many stars – and, for me, to be in that group back then was a dream come true, but it was also nerve-wracking.

So I made the line-up for Harbour View's Premier League team in 2009 after being champions of the under-21's – which was the first in history for the Harbour View under-21 team. I guess the reward for that was being moved to the senior team.

While I was experiencing my football dream, I was also working as an accounting clerk at my Dad's company. In Jamaica, football back then did not provide a steady enough source of income to be considered a lucrative pursuit. Football didn't pay enough to cover all my expenses. I was living with my mother and sister at the time. My sister was going to school; my mom didn't have a steady job, so I was the breadwinner, working and playing football.

I had to find a way to juggle two jobs for most of my early football career. I lived in Portmore, so I used to wake up early, get dressed for my accounting job, and travel for an hour in traffic to Kingston. If I had a morning training session, I would head to Harbour View first.

I was the only one on the team with a second job. So I would go to Harbour View for training when required. After training, I would take a shower, get dressed, and head to Downtown Kingston. I would take public transportation from there to Old Hope Road; sometimes it would be more than one bus, depending on the route I took. That was my routine.

Sometimes we had to train twice in one day, so I would head back to train after work and then go home to Portmore in the night. That was a very exhausting schedule.

Looking back at it now, I realize why I made the choices I did. I wanted a better life. I wanted to achieve my dreams. The routine was exhaustive, and it prevented me from playing at my best, but I felt I had no choice. I had to take a second job to help my mother with my sister as well as manage my own life. That was a really difficult time for me, but because I persisted and pressed through all that, I was afforded the opportunities that came my way.

Many in my position would have quit their pursuit of football and stuck with the option that provided more financially, but I couldn't bring myself to do that. I believed my purpose was football; I had a deep passion for it, and I refused to let it go, so whatever I needed to do was the price I was willing to pay, and I knew that one break was all I needed. It didn't happen overnight, but persistence always brings results.

Winning my award for "Best Eleven/Striker"
in the 2017 season in the Vleague.

Playing for the Jamaica National Football Team
(The Reggae Boyz) Against South Korea in 2015.

CHAPTER 3

My Idol: My Mentor

I didn't have perfect parents, nor did I grow up under the perfect family structure. My parents were as human as anyone else, so they made mistakes. When I was twenty-eight years old, my Dad told me that if he could turn back the hands of time, he would not break up with my mom. Regardless of the many arguments they had, he wished he had stuck with it. It felt good to hear that, especially now that I am married. Marriage comes with conflict, and I have seen a lot of conflict and have engaged in many arguments with my wife. We argue a lot, but I have never even had the thought of looking on the other side of the fence. And even if it is true that it is greener, I don't want to know.

My dad is the best, and none of his wrong decisions can change my perspective of him. He wasn't around physically while I was growing up, but he made sure I had a role model. He brought groceries, gave us lunch money for school, and if I needed the occasional funding for something, I could always depend on him to provide.

I initially thought my life was hard, but I had friends who didn't know their father at all and didn't have anyone for financial support. Dad could have turned his back completely on us, but he did not. He was an accountant. He had his own business. He always told stories of him and his brother sharing shoes to go to school on different shifts. I knew his life wasn't a bed of roses growing up either.

On occasion, dad would take me to his office, and I had that special feeling of being the Boss' son by how I was treated by clients and employees. My stepmom was another story. I think I had the kind of stepmom who tried everything to ensure that her husband would have nothing to do with the children before her. I would call the house on several occasions, and she would tell me Dad was not there. I would call grandma, and she would call the same number and receive a call back from Dad. Those were times when Dad was late with groceries or lunch money, so it was a matter of urgency.

My advice to stepmoms and stepdads today is to remember that children don't forget anything, especially how they are treated. It took me a long time to forgive, and even though I believe I have forgiven my stepmom for the times I felt hurt by her actions, the pain is still there. I can't stop myself from writing this, and I shouldn't have to hide the truth. I am a broken child in a big man's body, and maybe this is my therapy. Writing helps me release the pain.

Dad was my idol, my mentor. I learned a lot from him about life and the choices we have to make from time to time. I learned that hard work pays off, and we can go for what we desire and see it become a reality. I learned that life can be lived without regret if we never stop trying and don't give up. It's always good to have a father to look up to, and I can't imagine what my life would be if he was totally missing in action.

I love you, Dad.

CHAPTER 4

Crossroads of Life

I remember once a female friend sent me a message to ask for relationship advice. Apparently, her boyfriend was at a crossroads she had heard me share about because I was in the same position. He was leaving high school and was heading for University but going to University meant that he would have to stop playing football. Juggling between the University of the West Indies and getting to training would be a major issue. He loved football, but there comes a time when we have to be real with ourselves and face the reality that not everyone makes it. According to the statistics, less than 1% of those who love playing football, and desire to pursue it as a profession actually make the cut.

When I left Greater Portmore high school in 2003, I didn't want to stop my education. I wanted to move on to sixth form, but Greater Portmore did not have a sixth form. I had a pass in two subjects, and that could not get me into college, or into sixth form at another school. I would need to get passes in at least four more subjects in order to go to sixth form or college.

I had played on a team against the Calabar Football Team, and the coach told me that he wanted me to come and play for Calabar Manning Cup. What I did next was register for Calabar to attend an extended fifth form, which I had to do to qualify for sixth form. I was told by the Coach that if I passed four subjects, I would be able to go to sixth form, but I would have to sit out one full year of football to focus on studying. If I did manage to pass four additional subjects, I would then go to sixth form and play Manning Cup for Calabar. That would have placed my name on the local scene, as it does for many local prominent high school football players. It wasn't an easy choice. I was seventeen years old, and my educational pursuit was always a financial struggle. Sometimes, there was no lunch money or food in our refrigerator. I did attempt to start doing the extra classes, but after the first day, I called my dad while still on the school grounds, and I told him I was coming to work for him. I could not continue to struggle financially in the name of trying to get into college.

I started working at Dad's accounting company and made twenty-five thousand Jamaican dollars my first month. I felt like a seventeen-year-old millionaire. I was able to buy groceries for our house. The cupboards weren't empty anymore. I decided to work and chase my dream after work, and that became my routine. I woke up at 5 a.m. each morning, and I was ready to go at 6 a.m. to catch a bus from Portmore to Half Way Tree or Downtown. I would take a taxi to Old Hope Road, where my Dad's office was. I had no accounting experience, but I did get a pass in Accounts with a Grade 2. Dad taught me everything he could.

When I just started working as an accountant, I was playing the under 21's for Tivoli Gardens in 2008. My life's routine became work and training. I was always tired, but I was more motivated than tired. I told my female friend that if her boyfriend believes in his dream, then I don't see any reason why he should not chase after it. I knew it would be difficult balancing football training and College, but I also believe that having a real passion for something can drive a man beyond his limits. The most successful and greatest among us are more than willing to pay whatever the cost is of seeing a dream fulfilled. We only get one life. We pass by this way only once, so I believe we should make proper use of it.

In 2009, when the football season came around, I was very excited. I was playing for the Harbour View Football Club. It was my first game as part of the senior team, and I was picked to travel to Mexico to play in the Concacaf Champions League. We played against Pumas. That was my first time leaving Jamaica for an international football game and I was lucky enough to play as a substitute in the game.

We lost the game. I think the score was 3-0, but the international experience was good enough for me. It made me more confident, and I was a few steps closer to my dream of playing football outside of Jamaica.

The nature of having a dream is that sometimes there are hiccups. I had several games after my overseas experience, and in one of those games, I was injured. I twisted my ankle badly. I was out for two months. Things went a bit downhill following that injury. I wasn't at my best when I recovered from my injury, so I wasn't getting much play time. The season started in September of that year and, by December, I wanted to leave Harbour View because I felt like it wasn't working out.

I was a young player on a senior team, among some of the best players, and because I wasn't getting as much play time as I thought I should have, I had spoken with the coach, who was a Brazilian. I knew I was good enough to be playing regularly, and I guess I didn't have enough patience to wait my turn. I told the coach that I wanted to leave Harbour View because I wasn't being used to my full potential. He was a bit upset and told me he wanted me to stay because I was really talented, and he encouraged me to keep working hard.

I had planned to speak with the manager about leaving, and the coach stopped me. He told me to stay and be patient. I guess everything happens for a reason because the following year I signed my first contract in Russia and that was a dream come true. I was so excited. I called my mom and dad back home and told them I got the contract. It came in the local papers. All my friends were blowing me up. Everyone was excited.

I often reminisce about the moment I was in the Russian office signing that contract. No one can understand the joy I felt. I was twenty-one years old.

One month before that moment, I was standing at a bus stop in Greater Portmore. Sometimes the buses used to be so packed that I had to stand from Portmore to Kingston, Downtown or Half Way Tree. To be standing on a bus for an hour was awful. I would sometimes have to walk from Half Way Tree to New Kingston just to have enough money to purchase lunch. To leave all of that and end up in Russia, in the Premier League, no one could truly understand that feeling. All those sacrifices I had made working full time and playing pro football had brought forth its reward. All the crossroads I had to endure in my life had finally led me to exactly where I wanted to be, and that, I believe, is the nature of life and the experiences we have.

When I signed that contract, my first game was against CSKA Moscow, which was one of the biggest teams in the Russian Premier League. We lost that game 2-1, but I was voted in the top five best players of the game. This was my first international football game where I was a starter.

Despite my good fortune, I slowly started to realize there was another side to Russia. I experienced racism and other situations, which changed my life.

One day I was leaving the supermarket with my groceries, and three guys attacked me, calling me a *Nigger*, and started punching me. I had to leave my groceries and race back to the hotel where the team was staying. I was surprised and scared. It was a very traumatic experience. Because of that incident, I decided to research racism in Russia on the internet and saw a lot of videos of blacks and Asians being attacked. They also said that it wasn't safe to travel solo in Russia as a black person. I was so surprised. Sometimes, it is our ignorance that opens the door to certain experiences that could have easily been averted. But, it is also true that experience teaches one wisdom.

I left Jamaica at the age of twenty-one. I had never experienced a racial problem, not even when I had traveled to the United States, so this whole subject of racism took me by surprise.

I spent five to six months in Europe before returning to Jamaica. When I returned home, I went back to playing football and my 9-5 accounting job, after seeing my dream come to an end at such a short time. I decided I was done with international football, based on my experiences.

I was intent on working as an accountant for my dad and following in his footsteps. I would only play football for the fun of it. I loved football, and I could not give it up entirely. If I couldn't do it professionally, I would do it as a sport. But my passion for football had different plans for my life.

First Jamaican player to start a game in the Russian Premier League history. In these pics, I'm playing against the two biggest clubs in Russia; Zenit St. Petersburg and CSKA Moscow in 2009.

CHAPTER 5

Football System

The Football System had its good and its bad, as does everything else. It seems that with everything to get to greener pastures, one must pass through chaos. I have two boys who are half Jamaican and half Russian and, even though I love Jamaica, the system that I had to come up through was such an unfair one that I wonder if I will ever allow my kids to go through the same. It can be literal hell. It is not like track and field, where once your running time is good, no one can hold you out. Football is a team sport, and there are coaches who decide who plays and who stays on the bench.

I have played for the best local teams in Jamaica—Tivoli Gardens, Harbour View, Portmore United and Arnett Gardens, but it wasn't until I moved to Harbour View in 2008 that I realized how challenging the system can be. It's all about who benefits more financially. I guess it's always about the money, right?

I had just finished playing my first under-21 season for Tivoli Gardens, which was my first Premier League team. I finished with fourteen goals and was named the top scorer for my team. We finished second behind Portmore United, and the team had left just one week before the start of the season. I wanted to play as a striker, and they only wanted me as a defender because of my size. I was tall and strong. I couldn't argue with them back then because I was unknown. Most of the people around me didn't even know my surname. I didn't attend a prominent high school, so nobody knew me.

When I went to Portmore United, there were players such as Steven Morrissey, and the Wolfe Brothers. They were my friends and, at that time, if I said I thought I was better than them, everyone would consider me mad. But I did believe in my heart that I was the best player on the team, but no one saw it that way. So I spoke with the manager, and he understood my perspective, and for that, I always had respect for him. He was also a member of the Jamaica Football Federation (JFF). Even when I moved on to represent Jamaica, he didn't hold my decision to leave his team against me. I am not sure he even remembered me.

I moved from the Tivoli under-21 to Harbour View, and after playing just one game for Harbour View, I didn't score. Yet when the next under-23 squad was called for Jamaica, I was included. I was surprised, not because I didn't deserve it, but because I knew it was well overdue. I wasn't in the right club for the right people to benefit, then I figured it all out. All the heads of JFF at the time were connected to two of the local teams: Harbour View and Portmore United. I am not accusing anyone; I just found it ironic that as soon as I went to Harbour View, I was in the National Program. That was when I figured out why they hadn't called me from Tivoli Gardens, knowing that if I was to be sold overseas, those in charge of the 'System' wouldn't benefit from it financially. I can name thousands of players before me, from most of the inner-city clubs, who didn't get their chance for that same reason. Some did, but not enough.

I do not hate anyone for what has happened throughout my career. Everything has its purpose and reason. God had already written my script, so I believe He placed me in all the right environments for me to sit and write about it all today.

My Dad once said that if I had stayed and played for Portmore United as a defender, I would have been signed to England ages ago. Football is all I have. The way I express myself with the ball is a gift from God that I am grateful for. If I'm not dribbling and scoring goals, then I'm not happy. I didn't want to be an unhappy footballer with money.

The journey to our dreams has many crossroads, and we must learn to navigate our way through them. How we get to our destination is often shrouded in mystery, and it takes patience and faith to press through. The culmination of our gifts may not follow our pre-determined course of action and not every crossroad is labelled so we can easily choose our next move, but many times it would seem that some decisions are made for us to keep us on track, and we won't even realize it until we find ourselves standing in the fulfilment of our dream.

CHAPTER 6

Corruption

Let me be politically correct and address this issue like a man. There is a homosexual agenda permeating our society, and it affects every stratosphere of our lives. We work among them; enjoy the basic amenities of life side by side with them; support their businesses and buy their merchandise, etc., even without knowing. It is not an agenda that I support or endorse in any way, but it's an issue that is a little difficult to ignore.

I do not have one bone of hate in my blood, and I leave all judgment to God, as Romans 3:23 says, "All have sinned and fall short of the glory of God." I am a heterosexual man, and that's my stance. The problem I have with the homosexual agenda is the way it influences and plays a significant role, through gender preferences, in the selection of a team. If I made a calculated guess, I would say that homosexuals hold very influential positions in every area of society, and I think this is public knowledge. I know players who have had to leave Jamaica and are not able to return home because they were trying to find a shortcut in life. They are not homosexuals by nature but may have compromised in order to be placed on a team. While many people, in all areas of life, may have experienced success in this way, I believe only God can guarantee true success.

If you believe you were born gay or you naturally think you are gay, I have no problem with you. I don't judge. I would like to share a story of my own experience. I did something many years ago that I still regret today. I did reach out to the player that I offended and ask for his forgiveness. I was young and growing up in Jamaica, where we were raised with a very homophobic mentality. I have traveled the world and met gay people and, to be truthful, they have never approached me to do any harm. I have grown to see the world for what it is, so I know people want to live their lives the way they see fit. I am presently in an interracial marriage, and I have met white guys who don't support my marriage. I have lost black friends, mostly females, because I chose to marry a white woman. I always find it strange how Jamaicans are more willing to kill a homosexual while allowing a gunman to walk free. But who am I to judge the life one chooses to live.

About eleven years ago, I was a part of a local team where a specific player was always bullied by the rest of my teammates because he had fallen into the hands of a homosexual coach. Everybody knew, except me it seems, but I was eventually made aware of it. One day we were training, and this player kept losing the ball. Without thinking, I said to the player, *"Is it because you are sleeping with the coach why you are messing up our game?"* That comment cost me my starting spot for the rest of that season, and I was so angry at the time. The player reported me to the coach and told him what I said. It wasn't really a surprise to anyone, as most players in Jamaica and even non-homosexual coaches knew of these cases, but no one was brave enough to talk on the matter because it might cost them their jobs. I understand that. People have their families to feed.

A couple of years later, I saw that player, and what I did really changed me. I was in Kingston at a public place with my wife, close to where I used to work as an accountant, when I saw him. I went up to him and told him I was sorry for the way I treated him back then. It was immature of me. What he said to me really changed the way I thought about him. He told me that he was at that club since the age of ten years old and as he was about to start high school, the coach preyed on him. He didn't go much further into detail, and, frankly, he didn't have to. I started to think of my own children. We can be so neglectful letting our kids out into this world. The player said he had forgiven me a long time ago.

I didn't get a chance to talk with him after that, but I felt better. I was given the opportunity to fix or try to fix what I had said years ago. It's hard to summarize the message I want people to get from this because of the sensitive nature of this issue, but I pray you can take something away from what I have said.

Corruption exists at all levels, and our children will have to face up to it at some point in our lives when we are not around as parents. We may think we are doing our kids a favor by keeping them in the dark, but unless we educate them properly about the hell that exists in our world today and teach them how to respond to whatever may come their way, they may end up walking down the wrong path.

Our role as parents is great, and we have a responsibility to properly train up the next generation. If we are ever going to see a corrupt free society, there must be a generation that will stand up to what is not right and be adamant that they will not have any part in it. Success in life must be earned the right way, and shortcuts should be avoided.

CHAPTER 7

Pursuing the Dream

In the words of the great Martin Luther King, "I have a dream…" and I never gave up on that dream, because I saw my dad working seven days a week to see his dream fulfilled, and he never gave up. My mom had two children and no steady job, and she never gave up. So it was in my blood not to give up.

I have never met anyone who worked harder than my dad. As stated before, he is an Accounting Clerk and the CEO of his own company. He started that company from nothing, and I take my hat off to him for what he has accomplished. He had so many mouths to feed, being a father of four children and two step-children, but he never once ran away from his responsibilities. I am the older of his children, and I was blessed to get an opportunity to work side by side with him for seven years. I saw how much work he put in, and I believe he barely slept because the workload would often accumulate. He had a lot of clients, and no matter how much pressure he was under, he never stopped working. I used to watch him carefully, and he was my greatest motivation to not give up on my dream. He knew how to get things done and taught me the valuable lesson of pursuing my dream.

Dad got things done and still found time to make his children happy. I took that from him into my football career. No matter what, I never quit. Many times, I was tempted to throw in the towel, but I didn't. I would always remember my Dad and found the inner motivation to continue. He never quit, and one day my own children will say that about me.

Mom was equally resilient as well. She sacrificed it all for her children like every mother should. When there was nothing, she found something. She always found a way to ensure that we had what we needed. I think mothers are magicians. They can make a meal out of nothing.

Mom was strong, and she wasn't afraid to tell us like it is. She chose to go hungry many times, so we could have something to eat. Though we were kids, she told us the truth about life and what to expect along the journey. She gave us the real version of life. I grew up with all that information in mind, so I knew that life would not be easy. I knew I had to take care of myself and anyone I was given the responsibility to care for. I learned from a young age not to be too dependent on anyone, and it was my responsibility to make something of myself. I had friends who were sheltered by their parents through life, and when they became adults, it was too late for them to handle the issues of the world. This world is not for weak people who give up at the first sign of failure. I have failed a thousand times, and that is why I succeeded. The great Thomas Edison failed thousands of times before he succeeded in inventing the light bulb. He is famous for this quote, "*I have not failed 10,000 times. I have not failed once. I have succeeded in proving that those 10,000 ways will not work. When I have eliminated the ways that will not work, I will find the way that will work.*"[1]

---

[1] http://larryferlazzo.edublogs.org/2011/06/11/what-is-the-accurate-edison-quote-on-learning-from-failure/

Personal information	
Full name	Errol Anthony Stevens
Date of birth	9 May 1986 (age 32)
Place of birth	Kingston, St. Andrew, Jamaica
Height	1.91 m (6 ft 3 in)
Playing position	Forward
Club information	
Current team	Hai Phong

Senior career*			
Years	Team	Apps	(Gls)
2005–2009	Harbour View	3	(1)
2009	→ FC Khimki (loan)	3	(0)
2011–2012	Arnett Gardens	9	(7)
2013–2014	Saraburi	33	(16)
2015–	Hai Phong	78	(39)

I thank my parents for this valuable lesson of never giving up. They taught me the good and bad of life, and it made me the man I am today. I learned to accept life and the struggles that come with it. If I cried as a youngster, it brings me great joy today because all the good and bad of life growing up contributed to my completion.

I am now playing pro football in Vietnam, where I have the opportunity to put into practice everything I learned from my parents. The name of my team is "Hai Phong" and I have scored thirty-nine goals so far (See career stats above)

When I first arrived in Vietnam in 2011, there were twenty-two other players trying out for three open positions. These men were from all over the world – Brazil, Germany, France, and Spain. On our lunch break, we started talking to each other. I found out that some of them had even played in the Champions League.

I met these players at the try-outs and sent them a friend request on Facebook. I quickly realized that they were coming from Europe and had played for clubs all over the world. I remember this African I met. I found a picture of him with international footballer Ronaldo on the field in the Champions League.

At the end of the day, a lot of players are out there trying to make something of themselves, and it's not easy. So when you get a chance, it is necessary to put some of your pride aside and be willing to work hard for what you want. There are many players in Jamaica who would love the opportunity, even players from Brazil and Argentina as well, where footballers are produced by the second. In these countries, they are greeted with football as soon as they are born.

It is the same as any other job market. There are a lot of workers, in this case, players, and just a few jobs, so everyone must work hard and even consider other options for getting where they want to go. Growing up, I never thought I would be playing in Vietnam. I knew nothing about Vietnam until

I got here. The uncertainty of not knowing where our paths and decisions will take us can cause us to turn back or not try at all. I could have used my ignorance of this country as an excuse not to pursue my dream, but I decided to go along for the ride, and I have little regret today.

If someone is reaping success from the hard work they have put in, you cannot judge them. I talk about this all the time. When I left Jamaica for Thailand in 2013, I left Jamaica with $50 in my pocket. My fellow teammates, Dickoy Williams, and Kemar Daley, were there with me and we saw that the journey was going to be a rough one. It was going to be hell.

Dickoy and I drove five hours for a try-out that our agent had set up. When we got there, the team told us we couldn't train. The agent told us we were expected but when we got there, we couldn't even enter the stadium. They said they didn't know anything about us. They turned us back, and we had to drive five hours back home.

Dickoy and I were ready to pack up and go back to Jamaica, but when we got back to our rooms, I started thinking that it might not be so wise to go back to Jamaica since I had no opportunities to go back to. I decided to stay and pursue.

I ended up getting signed because a team was looking for a forward and not a defender. I signed for a team in Thailand for US$2000. After I signed the contract, the boss showed me the apartment I would be staying in, and it was worse than even the worse I had ever been in Jamaica. It was an empty room – no bed, no furniture, nothing. It was an old building. All that was there was a *'Tatami'* mat that Asians sleep on. I slept on it for six months.

I remember one day a close friend said to me when I was injured in 2012, *"Jabba (my nickname), I'm glad I'm not a baller anymore because you got nothing out of it."*

I was shocked that he said that. It was as if he felt good that he had abandoned his dream because of my own failure. This is someone who I played football with since we were kids. I knew I couldn't give up. I knew I had to press beyond the perception and talk of the naysayers around me. It is funny that many times your haters are within your own inner circle.

Pursuing my dream was no walk in the park, but I came through. I persevered and endured the difficulties that presented themselves, and I believe I can say like Job, "But he knows the way that I take; when he has tested me, I will come forth as gold" (Job 23:10 – NIV).

In 2014, I helped Gulf Saraburi Fc get promoted to the Thai Premier League for the first time in the club's history, one of the most memorable moments in my career. Here I am celebrating with my teammates after beating Anthong Fc 3-2. I scored 1 and assisted 1 on that night.

*"Playing in Saraburi, Thailand back in 2014,
in front of my home fans. I cherish these memories."*

"Playing in VLeague, in Vietnam."

*"Currently playing in the VLeague in Vietnam for Hai Phong FC.
This is my fourth season at the club."*

"I was given this photo by the fans of my club in 2016 after helping the team to finish second in the league. We almost won the league. I was injured for more than half of that season. My biggest regret was not lifting the cup."

Totchtawan Sripan is the best Coach I know. I learned so much from him, and this was the turning point in my career. I thought I knew all there was to know about football until I met this man. The tactical aspects of my game completely changed. He is honored in THAILAND as the greatest midfielder in the country's history. During his career, playing for clubs in Thailand, Vietnam, and Singapore, he played as central midfielder or attacking midfielder. Totchtawan was a longstanding member of the Thailand national team, playing from 1992 to 2008.

CHAPTER 8

My Soul Mate

I want to include my wife in this story because she is a true soldier. When I met her, all I had in the room was a bed and a small TV. There was no kitchen, and she still chose to come and live with me. It was January 2014, and she stayed with me in that condition.

I met my wife online in October 2013 on her birthday. But we didn't physically see each other until January 2014. I was living in a room in an old building with only a bed and a television. I believe I was able to buy a refrigerator shortly after she came. It was not the ideal condition under which to start a relationship, but you will understand why I love my wife. When she came, and I saw that she was serious about staying with me, regardless, I asked her what she was doing with me because I knew she could do better. I said to her, *"Swaggy (my name for her), I only make $2000. What if I should lose my job one day because of an injury or something else?"*

She saw me collecting US$2000 every month, and after paying all my bills, I only had US$500, and I still sent US$300 to my mother in Jamaica. Swaggy kept the US$200 for our savings. That US$300 I sent to my mother paid the bills in Jamaica for her and my sister.

So I was playing professional football, making a profit of US$500, and sending more money to my mother than what I kept for myself.

At this time, in Thailand, it took me an hour to get to training. I have Thai friends who can testify to that; one hour to training, one hour back on a US$2000 paycheck.

I had a lot of respect for Swaggy because she endured the discomfort with me through all of that – something a lot of women wouldn't do. I never had any money to give her. So one day I said to her, *"Swaggy, if anything should happen and I lose my job, I wouldn't be able to take you to Jamaica because I have no money. I would have to pay for my ticket home. The most I could do for you is get your ticket to go back to Russia."*

She told me she loved me, even if she had to work at Burger King. I don't want to say she was naïve, but that didn't make sense to me. I was really concerned, because sometime before that, she needed to have Lasik surgery for an eye condition. I found out the surgery was US$2500 – far more than what I was getting for my pay.

Swaggy messaged her mother for the money and, within 3-4 days, she received the money. I told Swaggy there was no one in my life I could get that kind of favor from. I really had to ask her why she was with me. When she explained how she really felt about me and the love she had for me, I found her irresistible.

I had bought a motorbike when I met her, and we had two accidents while riding it. We ended up in the hospital on one occasion. We were both hurt because it was my first time riding a motorcycle. I felt awful our first night home from the hospital because of all the pain she was in. As I look back, we can laugh at those occurrences now because we are in a better position. But at the end of the day, life can go up, or it can come down. We are not rich, but we are not where we used to be either. The bills are paid, we own our home, and we have a car.

After all I have been through, all I have to say to the people talking about me is, "God go with you. God bless you."

The reason I give so many details is that I want people to know the full story. It wasn't an easy journey for me, but I got what I needed at all the right intervals in life to take me a little further.

I remember one day when Swaggy and I just started going out. It was raining heavily when we were about to head back home. In Thailand, when it rains, the roads are full of water soon after it starts. I didn't want to take Swaggy on the bike so far in the heavy rain and risk her getting sick.

Thailand isn't a poor country, and most of my teammates were well off. I had teammates that drove an Audi, BMW, and Chevrolet – those big brands. They had their families. Thailand is better off than Vietnam in terms of the professionalism of the football. The players are well-paid. I'm not saying Vietnam doesn't have money, but I found Thailand more professional to some extent.

So here we were, and the rain was coming down hard. I asked Swaggy to get a drive with one of my teammates in their car. He lived close to our apartment. Swaggy refused, and that caused a big argument. I got mad because I didn't want her in the bad weather with me on the motorcycle. She wouldn't have it, and she rode with me on the bike, in the pouring rain. The entire time we were heading home, I kept thinking about something Twins of Twins said about testing your woman by driving your car on empty to see if she would help you push it. Swaggy could have been in an Audi or a BMW, but she chose to ride on a bike with me.

When she just came to Thailand, she could choose to be with any guy she wanted. A lot of my teammates liked her. I don't blame them, because she is beautiful. It sounds petty, but it's the truth. She's my wife, and I love her. She's the most beautiful soul I know. She could have gone with anyone she wanted.

My teammate said I motivated him with the steps I took to get married. Maybe it's not a big deal for most people, but for us ghetto boys, it's not something we put much emphasis on, but being honest, when you find something you know you can't live without or someone who makes you want to live more, then why not keep that person around. It took all my savings to marry my wife. We got married on February 20, 2015, just a couple months after moving to Vietnam. The US$200 a month that we saved for eighteen months, plus money I had earned for helping my Division One Team in Thailand to the Premier League, was totally depleted by our wedding.

As I look back, I know I was crazy in love. If I had been injured during that time, or something came up requiring finances, I would have been in trouble because I was completely broke. But I wasn't thinking like that. I think the systems of this world wants us to think like that, to always be in fear and live life from that perspective. I have always been a man of faith. I knew that no matter which direction the pendulum swung, God had a desire for me to succeed.

I moved to Vietnam in 2015. It was a much better condition than what we had gotten used to in Thailand. We were given a couple weeks off, so we flew to Jamaica. It was her first time on the island, and while she was excited, I was extremely nervous. I was nervous because she met me in Thailand, so she had no idea where I was living prior to that. She had never seen where I was from. She was aware because of our conversations, and we had been together for over a year, but her actually seeing it was enough to make a grown man sweat. I kept thinking, *Would she want to still be with me after seeing where I'm from?* I was still under the same roof with my mom and sister. Yes, I had dreams of building my own space upstairs, but life took me down a different path.

We landed in Jamaica, and she loved everything. We were young and in love, and I feel proud that we didn't let material things or anything, for that matter, stop us from being together. I thought the environment would be below her conditions as compared to Russia, where she is from. Russian is a first world country, with the most beautiful buildings and designs. How could she leave that, and love a little island with all its bad roads, trees, derelicts, smog, etc. I learned something from her; God made everything beautiful.

We went to my home in Greater Portmore, and we stayed in my old room. It was a Portmore quad room, and she didn't seem out of place or show any signs of doubt. She just wanted to marry the guy she fell in love with.

We had already booked everything from before we landed thanks to my sister Jody and my cousin Janique. My cousin worked at Secrets Resort in Montego Bay, and she got us a good deal on getting married there. There was only one problem; I didn't have enough money to invite all my family. We actually had a very small wedding. I married my girlfriend, Ekaterina Nikiforova, aka 'Swaggy.'

It wasn't as easy as it seemed to get married. My wife was a Russian citizen, and she required more documents to get married. I was a Jamaican, so it was easy for me. The good thing is, Secrets Resorts was used to that kind of arrangement, so they knew exactly what was needed and could direct us accordingly. It was a good decision to go there for our wedding, and it is a beautiful place. It was a dream come true.

Prior to coming to Jamaica, we had already bought our rings and clothes from Thailand. Our wedding rings weren't the fancy type that I wished we could afford. There was just not enough money, so we had to budget for everything. I didn't know anything about Secrets Resort before I went there to get married, but I could tell that most, if not all, of the people there had money. It was just one of those places that you had to be able to afford in order to go, and we were not on the same financial level as the other guests.

The day before the wedding, we met this couple. They were really happy and surprised to see a young couple like us getting married at the resort. The husband told me they got married also when they were young, and they didn't have anything. He was now a very big Real Estate Agent, with millions of dollars. He didn't have to tell me, because I knew just by looking at them that they had money. I was comforted by his story, and it gave me hope. I had a practice of looking and planning ahead, and I knew that as a Jamaican football player on a National Team, I was in the limelight, and it would just be a matter of time.

I was now an International Player in an International relationship. It was not easy, and it's not about what people thought or said about us. It was our responsibility to make our marriage work. Our marriage came with a high maintenance rating. All my wife's family is in Russia, so she has to visit her mom from time to time, when we can afford it. We both knew that we were walking a road that not many survive together, but we did it. We got married, and it was the best day of my life. I still get chills thinking about it. My wife is an angel and seeing her walking down that aisle did something to my soul.

When people look at us, all some see is color. I see two souls entwined for eternity. I know what is inside my wife more than anyone on this planet, and we are far from perfect, but we both want the best for each other.

Faith is a wonderful thing. It is said that Faith can move mountains, and that's what I want you to get from this chapter; have faith.

At the publishing of this book, it has been three wonderful years of marriage, two awesome children, and a home, and we are still deeply in love as if we met only yesterday. God has been so good to us.

Family photo. I am holding Lionel. My wife is holding Daniel.

Our wedding day at Secrets Resort in 2015. My sister,
Jody-Ann, is behind me. My cousin, Janique, is on my wife's side.

The Stevens family celebrating Christmas in Vietnam.

The Stevens family going to the finals of
the under-23 AFC cup in Vietnam.

The Stevens family, enjoying a lovely day in the park in Vietnam.

CHAPTER 9

To My Children

My kids are my world, and they have given meaning to my life. I am a better man because of them.

I was raised in a broken home. My parents got divorced when I was five years old, and it felt like my world came crashing down on me. I knew in my heart that the struggles I had growing up was not something I wanted for my children. I have never shared this until now, but there is a letter my mom let me read when I was small that brought tears to my eyes. My stepmom wrote a letter talking about me and my sister, and not in a good way. We were babies caught up in the issues of divorce, but the words used to describe us was nothing I would tell my worst enemy. The only part of her letter I will share here is that she said we would turn out to be nothing. I was always told to not talk badly about other people's children because it may fall upon your own, but I guess not everyone takes this advice.

That letter, and those harsh words, made me want to prove people wrong all my life. People always wonder why I am so confident and why I am so unbreakable. It's because I can't give up. I just can't. I am the child nobody expected anything from. I am the friend nobody wanted to be friends with when I was young because it wasn't profitable. I was just a kid who loved football, and that's the greatest gift my dad ever gave to me.

When my dad left, he took my heart with him. I cry writing this, and I'm also afraid of him reading it. But Dad, if you ever read this, I want you to know that I saw you as the best dad in the whole world. We all make mistakes. Some relationships work; some don't. I don't know why you and mom were among those that didn't, but both of you were needed to get me here, and that was enough. Imagine what the world would be like today without me. No child wants to lose their father or see their parents break up. Dad, you are my world, and no matter how you and mom fought or what was said, as a young boy, you could do no wrong.

I remember some weekends I would call my dad to come and get me, and he said okay. I would sit on my little bridge in 2 East Greater Portmore waiting as soon as I got home from school, sometimes as early as 8 p.m. I watched and waited to see that black van or I would call him, and he would say, *"Junior, I'm on the way."* My mom would shout from the house, calling me an idiot for allowing dad to trick me into thinking he was coming; yet, every week I would be on that bridge waiting. Maybe, somewhere deep in my heart, I wanted to prove to my dad that he should have never left. I wanted to be everything he was; a footballer and an accountant, although I didn't really like the latter, but my dad was an accountant, so I wanted to be one, simple as that. I share this story, so one day when my sons, Leo and Daniel, grow up, they won't make the same mistakes I did. I had to live with my mistakes. My dad is my idol, and I love him no matter what, and nothing could ever change that. We are best friends to this day.

Never envy someone for what they have. Things may be up for them now, but it could go down tomorrow. If it does go down, and you sit laughing at them, it still won't benefit you.

I am fighting a constant battle, ever fighting. It may look good now, and I give God thanks every day. Sometimes I cry when I'm home, hugging my kids or my wife. Sometimes she asks me why I'm crying. I just tell her I never thought my life would improve. I thought my life would always be hell.

I remember my time in Portmore Lane, Seaview, Greater Portmore. My life there wasn't pretty, but as I said, God is good. I'm still here fighting the battle, taking the journey one day at a time. Nothing is perfect, no matter how it may seem.

In another light, I could say it is perfect because I really don't need much. Even though things are getting better for me, I really don't need much. If I can afford to feed my children and my wife, I'm okay. I want it all, but if I don't get it all, I have enough, and I am truly grateful for where I am now. I don't take it for granted.

So at the end of the day, go out and work hard. Make the sacrifices for your benefit. Don't envy someone else and wish bad for them because it all starts from nothing. You must believe in yourself – no one else can do that for you. I believed in myself when I had nothing and even when I was discouraged, when I was injured, I still hang on to every thread of hope I could find in my heart. My children, the world may not believe in you, but know that I believe in you.

This was a family vacation. This is me and my son, Lionel, in Nha Trang, Vietnam.

My two lovely boys, Lionel and Daniel, Christmas photo shoot.

My son, Lionel, celebrating TET Lunar New Year
at school in Vietnam with two of his classmates.

My son, Lionel, dressed in Vietnamese traditional clothes.

Like father, like son ☺ Lionel at two years old.

My son, Daniel, riding around our home in Vietnam
on his bike. He is ten months old.

CHAPTER 10

My Wife's Story

To most people, and some of my friends, my wife is like a
mystery lady, like the main character in the movie *Dancehall
Queen*. She is from a city called Tyumen in Russia, and a lot
of people wonder how we met. I thought, maybe I should
share that story.

I met my wife on social media via a friend who I had met in
Russia when I was playing there. It was her 18th birthday,
and I had seen my friend posting a happy birthday message
to her. What caught my attention was her smile on the
birthday picture she posted. I never forgot that smile, and
I wanted to know who she was. Now, I consider myself
a brave guy, so I messaged her and said hello and happy
birthday. We started talking.

I shared my story of when I was going through my battles
and had just signed the contract to play in Thailand and
had to sleep in an empty building on a mat. I hadn't looked
at her profile yet to see that she was a dancer. When I saw
that, I started talking to her about teaching me to dance
one day. We had daily conversations. She was like my pen
pal. I would tell her stuff that I wouldn't tell anyone, and
she would do the same. I was having a rough time, and she
was having her own rough time. She lived with her mom
and had never met her dad since birth. She was in her first
year of University and was struggling with a lot of things
financially and emotionally. We found comfort in talking
with each other. I guess we both knew we were too far from
each other and we needed to get back to our own lives. I

knew nobody from her side, and she knew nobody from my side; our only connection was social media. So yes, there are some happy stories coming out of social media. It's not all negative.

We were social media friends for three months. Sometimes we did video calls and could talk for hours, and we did this for days. We spoke till one day she said she was looking forward to her break coming up. She had two weeks off from University, and I asked if she wanted to visit me in Thailand. I was falling in love with her every day in ways I could not explain because we had never met physically. Even if she did feel the same way, I wasn't in any financial position to tell her to leave Russia and come and live with me. I was a broke football player, starting over from the bottom of the bottom. She knew it all. That is all we would talk about. I would tell her about my failures, and it gave me comfort as she would tell me about hers. To my pleasant surprise, she took up my offer to come. I bought the tickets for two weeks, and I went to buy a bed, a television, and a refrigerator just to make the place look a bit more presentable.

I went to pick her up at the Bangkok Airport. The flight was three hours late, which only made me more anxious. It was her first time flying, her first time leaving her country. When she arrived, believe me, to this day we joke about it, we were utterly speechless. We had never seen each other in person and talking over a phone is a whole complete different situation.

We had shared with her friend the possibility of her coming to see me, and the friend was not supportive. I don't blame her with all the horror stories circulating. I guess her friend also didn't see the benefit of it at the time. She came anyway of her own will.

We were in a taxi heading back to my small city, Saraburi, which was a two-hour drive with the traffic. We started talking and couldn't stop. It was real. I knew it because I was never so open with anyone in my life, and, for those two weeks, I wished it would never end.

After two weeks, something made her decide not to go back home. I was angry and afraid and happy at the same time. I had no money to take care of her. I gave her my famous presidential speech, *"Ekaterina! If I lose my job today, I'm broke. I can't take you to Jamaica because I have nothing at home. I'm still living with my mom and sister, and even if I did take you back, the conditions are not what you are used to in Russia, and you are talking about giving up university! Are you serious?"* Her response was as crazy as her decision to stay, *"Even if I have to work at Burger King, I want to be with you."* The rest is history, as they would say.

We have two kids, so far. We just bought our first home, and our car is fully paid for. If that isn't Gods plan, then I don't what is. That's how I want my wife to be remembered, and for her grandchildren one day to know how great a woman she is. She taught me true courage. I feel invincible since she came into my life. Everything has been on the "up and up," as we Jamaicans would say. She made me want everything. I want the world and everything in it because I didn't want to lose her. If I was confident before, I am over-confident now.

The person you marry is really important. The one you fall in love with can set the tone for your life. My wife believed in me so much that I had no choice but to believe in myself. When I look at what we have accomplished together, I know God is watching over us.

On our wedding day at the beach in Montego Bay.

Picture-perfect moment from our wedding day.

The "Couple of the Year Award" goes to…Us!

Dancing to our song. The moments we never forget.

CHAPTER 11

How Vietnam Changed My Life

I once told my wife that when we move into our house in Vietnam for the first time, we will put a Vietnamese flag on the roof like all proud Vietnamese do. We may not be Vietnamese or look like Vietnamese, but Vietnam has given us everything. Everything we have achieved and own is because of Vietnam Football. Yes, God is the giver of all good things, but He has placed us in an environment where we could make enough money to change our lives.

Initially, we had a thought to build on to my mom's existing house in Jamaica, but now we were able to purchase our own house. Vietnam allowed us to have children. If we were unable to care for them financially, it wouldn't be possible, or we would have chosen not to have children. Our two boys, Lionel and Daniel Stevens, were born in Vietnam. They know no other home. My two-year-old, Lionel, is speaking Vietnamese at his school. I owe my life and accomplishments to Vietnam, and my prayer is always, *"Thank God for Vietnam."*

When I was first told by an agent to come to Vietnam to play professional football, I had no inclination that choosing to do so would impact my life so greatly. Vietnam has radically changed my life and will always hold a place in my heart. When we move back home after I retire, Vietnam will always be in my heart as the place I found my life.

We were meant to be together, and it would not be possible if it wasn't for life in Vietnam.

CHAPTER 12

A Word to the Wise

Sometimes God wants to bless you, but He has to weed out all the bad seeds, for example, some people, out of your life. I truly believe that because of some of the things we have been through, even the way we live sometimes can block our blessings.

When I was young, I was the typical Jamaican young boy, aka *'Balla'* as they would call us. That nickname would stick to anyone who is gifted with the football talent. Those who play football locally in Jamaica get huge ratings, and their lifestyles usually include partying and a lot of girls. I have known fellow peers in this sport, and I know we love the hype it brings, but slowly and surely, it has contributed in a big way to our demise. I am among the lucky few to have escaped that culture.

I was a part of the 2014 World Cup campaign for Jamaica. I was on the national team. I was just 26 years old, and a local player. I am one of the lucky few who got placed. All the players were being called from England and the United States. I dropped out after three games because I found out that I had a torn cartilage in my right knee, just prior to the game where Jamaica beat the United States of America in the National Stadium. I was sitting in the stands with my sister, sad but happy at the same time. I recalled, just weeks prior, I was on the bench coming on as a substitute against Antigua. That's life, I thought. I blamed that injury up to this day on the lifestyle I was living. I was at every event.

People just expected me to show up. I was in every club in Kingston and, as I reflect, it is a significant contrast to how simple my life is today being married with responsibility. It makes me wish I was married back then, not to say married men don't party, but a family to feed does give you serious responsibilities and obligations to think about all the time. Back then, I was with every girl I could catch, and that also distracted me from my profession.

Every time I talk to a player back home who desires to go after their dream, I always advise them to make the sacrifices needed. I don't want them to fall into the same trap that I did. I was lucky enough to get a second chance after my injury.

The friends you keep around you are very important. I had a friend who would call me out to party every single time, even when I was injured. A couple months after my surgery, when I was home alone, and no one came to visit me out of the hundreds of friends I had, I saw him. He is the friend who told me that he was glad he stopped playing football. He said I had been trying for so many years and I didn't achieve anything from it. I never forgot those words, and I really am wondering what he's thinking to himself now. We are no longer friends, but I know he's out there watching. I did get something out of football; I got passion, experience, opportunities, and a fulfilled life. I could not have asked for more.

We can be who we want to be and achieve much, if we are willing to pay the price. It is said that where much is given, much is required, and there is no truer statement. Still, the message is a very simple one; if I can do it, so can you.

EPILOGUE

What I Have Learned

There is a reason for all the experiences that we have, and if we take the time to learn from them, we can walk away from any experiences wiser, and stronger. My life's experiences taught me wisdom that I would like to share with you. If you take away nothing else from my story, remember these valuable lessons. They may save you some time and accelerate your own personal pursuit of your dream.

The racism in Russia taught me strength. I learned to be proud of my blackness. I know that wasn't the intention of the racist people I encountered, but I became the best black man I could be. I learned to love me more.

When I first experienced it, I wanted to literally jump off my team hotel roof. I was 21 years old, young, alone, and afraid in a foreign country. I chose to embrace who God made me to be, and God makes no mistakes. Now, nothing can break me because of that experience. I took it into every area of my life, and people know when they meet me because I am very transparent in my actions and what I say. I fear nothing.

I think people who walk around with so much hate to fuel racism are the ones who need the most help and love. People may be asking how I could have faced racism and still end up marrying a Russian/White lady. Honestly, it was God's plan. I married her heart, not her skin, but for me, sometimes it is hard to speak pro black when your wife is white in the world that only sees life in shades. Having a white wife doesn't save me from racism. I have experienced more since we started dating. It puts pressure on us when we go out in the public arena because all eyes are on us, but we are living the dream, and I wouldn't trade my life for the world.

In Thailand, I learned that **it is okay to start small.** I had to literally start over when I got there, and I had nothing. I want people to shed their shame of humble beginnings and never forget where you are coming from. I signed a US$2000 contract in Thailand, and I had to live under the worst conditions of my life, but I knew where I wanted to go. I had a plan, and I may not have said it out loud, but I made an affirmation when I was leaving Jamaica to Thailand that I wouldn't go home until I was retired. Now, look at my life, considering that I left Jamaica with only US$50.

I want my generation back home to use my story as an example. There are too many who want the fast cash who are not willing to wait on God's timing. I am begging you to be patient. Anything God starts, He has the capacity to see it to completion.

In Vietnam, I learned that **your cultural background doesn't matter**. With a little effort and a healthy dose of courage, we can build our life anywhere.

When people hear 'Vietnam' what usually comes to mind is 'war.' But Vietnam is far more. I have learned a "way of life" here that I wish my home country would adapt. I have lived here for five years, and I have never heard a gunshot or seen anyone stabbed. Vietnam is like heaven for me. I had rented my own home, and I can leave it open. I can send my wife to pick up my kids and not worry. The Vietnamese people would say, *"com sau,"* which means *'no problem.'*

Jamaicans are known to use the phrase, *"No problem, man"* but the reality is, everything is a problem. In Vietnam, for example, I was riding my bike and I saw two people collide on their bikes and fall. If I was back home, the one who was wrong would probably have a big problem with the one who felt he was right. A fight would probably break out. But in Vietnam, they both picked up their bikes and seeing that no one was seriously hurt, and the damages were not bad enough to merit the law getting involved, they just moved on.

Vietnam has taught me to be calm and peaceful during times when I was usually very annoyed and aggressive. I would sometimes get angry for the smallest things, but over the years, I can honestly say that I have changed. I have become a better man because of the way of life in Vietnam. In this environment, nothing is more important than life.

In Jamaica, then and now, if you stepped on a man's shoes, it could cost you your life. We place greater emphasis on the value of material possessions than we do on human life, and I think that is just stupid. I blame my culture and country for the negative aspects of who I used to be, but I am hopeful that if I can change, anyone can experience the same change. We need to change our mentality and value human life. People are dying every day because we have no love for each other. We must change for the sake of our children's future. What legacy or inheritance do you really want to leave for your children? It's not enough that we choose a path, then say we don't want our children to walk that same path. What about leading and living by example?

I want to return home one day. There is no place like home. I don't necessarily want to live in another country. I will not put the full blame of our continual fall into degradation on the leaders of the country, because together, we must all find that place of love and mutual respect.

The greatest lesson I can leave with you is the lesson of our Lord Jesus Christ. Everything I have and who I am is because of Jesus. I don't argue my religion with people because I have nothing to prove to anyone. I know who

I have prayed to all my life, and He has always answered my prayers. Religion is so divided, but my stance is, if Buddha makes you live a peaceful life, then amen. If Allah makes you a peaceful man, then amen. We are all brothers and sisters, and we serve the same God, but we give him different names.

I want to raise my children to know Jesus because there is no life without Him. My faith was built on Him, and without that, I would have given up years ago. I live by this verse of Scripture:

> *Now faith is the substance of things hoped for, the evidence of things not seen. (Hebrews 11:1 – KJV)*

I prayed for the life I am living now, and I believed that one day it would happen. It doesn't matter what is happening in churches or how many pastors are making mistakes—never place your faith in man. Put your faith in God. The pastor is just as human as you are, and there is no good in man, really. Our best attempt at righteousness is like 'filthy rags.' Yet, there is a promise in Scripture that if God is for you, who can be against you (Romans 8:21). You cannot fail with God in your life, and I believe it is because of Him that I found success in life, despite the hell I had to walk through. The fire that doesn't consume you, will purge you.

Finally, be real and be true to yourself. Take counsel from others, but always listen to your own heart. You will find that, in life, when people can't do something they want to, or they find it difficult to pursue their own dreams, they will try to push your dreams aside as well. If I had listened to half the people who said I would never go pro, or never play for Jamaica, I would not be where I am today. I know that where I am now, will lead to an even bigger door opening for me in the future.

> *Brothers and sisters, I do not consider myself yet to have taken hold of it. But one thing I do: Forgetting what is behind and straining toward what is ahead. (Philippians 3:13 – NIV)*

I am the guy who went to Greater Portmore high school, now writing his own book. If that doesn't inspire you that you can become anything you want in this life, I don't know what will. If you can think it, know that it's possible. I am not afraid to dream anymore. I sometimes sit and think about a goal I can score. I sit and daydream about it, and then, just like that, I do it in a game. That's active faith at work.

So believe in yourself. Be confident in yourself. It's okay to have people to look up to; a pastor, teacher, parents, etc., but remember, they are not perfect. Look to God; believe in Him and believe in yourself, and everything you thought was impossible will flow into your life.

You may be going through hell now, but I know what's waiting for you on the other side, so don't stop. Keep moving. Keep dreaming. Keep believing and keep hope alive. One day soon, you will have your own story to tell.

This was Arnett's first senior Cup in seven years, and I was awarded MVP of the tournament. Another great achievement for me.

One day, I sat in the Stadium watching the Jamaica National Team play. I was dreaming about being a part of the team. That dream came through in 2010, and I feel honored to be in this picture, among the players on the starting line for the Reggae Boyz team.

This is the group of players that started the game that helped Saraburi Fc qualify for the Thai Premier League.

Connect with Errol Anthony Stevens

By Email:
Email: erroljahbastevens@gmail.com

On Social Media:
www.instagram.com/errolanthonystevens10
www.twitter.com/errolstevens
www.facebook.com/errolanthony.stevens
https://www.facebook.com/erroljahba7
www.youtube.com/erroljahbastevens

Please be kind to write a constructive review on *Amazon*.
Thank you in advance.

Made in the USA
Coppell, TX
26 March 2020

17727572R00069